# Paintbrush
# &
# Peacepipe:

## The Story of George Catlin

# Paintbrush

# &

# Peacepipe:

## The Story of George Catlin

*by Anne Rockwell*

ATHENEUM *1971* NEW YORK

*for* Hannah,
Elizabeth & Oliver

*The illustrations appearing in this book are adaptations, in sinopia pencil, of portraits and sketches George Catlin made while he was living and working among the Plains Indians of the West and other tribes.*

*A.R.*

# Paintbrush
# &
# Peacepipe:

## The Story of George Catlin

*Wi-jun-jon in Assiniboin clothing*

# chapter one

Some people seem to know from the day they are
born what it is they want to spend their lives doing.
Some people do not discover the things that really
interest them most until they are grown. And still
others gradually develop an interest that finally be-
comes the most important thing in their lives. George
Catlin was one of these. His interest in Indians, which
was eventually to take him all over the world and
to make him lose family, friends and livelihood, began
on a fine evening in the year 1805.

George was going to shoot a deer. He had decided
that. He was only nine years old, and, his father said,
much too young to handle a deer rifle. Nevertheless,
he had borrowed his older brother's rifle without telling anyone. And he and the rifle were hiding in the
forest near a salt spring where the deer came each

evening to lick. The sun was falling low behind the Pennsylvania woods as he lay hidden by a large bush. He hoped he had chosen a good spot, and he knew he had when a large buck with wide antlers came silently out of the forest into the little clearing.

George's hands trembled and shook with excitement as he grasped the trigger; his palms grew slippery with sweat. He tried to pull the trigger, but his hands trembled too much. He could not. All he could do was watch as the deer stood calmly licking at the salty rocks. Then, suddenly, a crashing sound filled the whole forest, and the deer fell dead. George looked down with amazement at his rifle. Had he fired it after all? No, the rifle was still cocked, ready to fire, and his wet palms slid clumsily down the cold and shining barrel.

Then, mysteriously and silently, a tall, brown-skinned man with long black hair stepped out of the forest, holding a rifle in his hand. He took a knife and deftly began to skin the deer.

Now George's hands trembled with terror instead of excitement. For he was sure that the man he was watching was an Indian. George had never seen an Indian, but he had heard tales of Indian raids. As he watched the man skin the deer, he pictured to himself how quickly and neatly the Indian could scalp him! But where had the Indian come from? In that part of Pennsylvania, near Wilkes-Barre, there were no Indians living. Years earlier many of them had been killed in battles with the white settlers, who had then been just moving into the area. The Indians who survived had been driven farther west, into lands that had never been farmed.

George watched, hardly daring to breathe, as the Indian finished his work, then sat down on a rock and took out a pipe. He lit it. Clouds of sweet-smelling, lavender smoke floated in lazy circles around his head. Evening coolness was falling over the woods, and everything was perfectly silent. All the daytime birds and insects had stopped their singing and buzzing. In the hush the Indian looked straight over to the bush where George lay hidden, and his eyes rested there. George did not dare turn his head away from the Indian's steady gaze, lest he make a sound. He stared unblinking into the Indian's eyes, certain that the man saw him.

And then, George could not believe what he felt; his breath came again, his hands grew steady, and his fear went away. Something he saw in the Indian's eyes made him feel strangely sure that he and the Indian could be friends. At that point the Indian stood up, lightly lifted the heavy buck across his shoulders, and, straight-backed and silent, disappeared into the forest.

George ran home. There he blurted out the story of the Indian to his father and some guests, even confessing to taking his brother's rifle. But the men sitting with his father laughed at him.

"It must have been a Gypsy," one said. "There've been Gypsies around lately."

George was sure the man was wrong. It *had* been an Indian. And it had been the most exciting thing, the most mysterious thing, that had ever happened

5

to him. But he knew better than to argue with a grown-up. Instead he went straight to his bed and collapsed, crying hard from the excitement and terror and relief of the day.

He was almost asleep when his mother came to his room. She stroked his forehead and whispered to him that she believed him. Relieved that someone thought him more than a fool, he told her the whole story, in every detail. He ended by saying that the Indian looked to him like a good man.

His mother smiled, and then she told a story. It had to do with something that had happened to her when she was a little girl. It was a strange story, one that George had never heard before. His mother said she didn't like to talk about it, for no one believed her. It always started arguments, so she had learned to keep quiet.

When she was younger than George, she said, her home had been raided by Indians. She and her mother had been taken away by the war party. They had been very frightened. But for several days they had lived, just the two of them, among the Indians. To their surprise, they had been given good things to eat and had been treated kindly. The Indians had spoken to them softly and politely. She had noticed that neither she nor any little Indian child was ever spanked, or even shouted at. Then, one day, the Indians had returned her with her mother, to her father. It had always seemed like a dream to Mrs. Catlin, and all her life she had wondered about it. When people talked about how evil and savage all Indians were, she had

6

wondered, but she had never seen any more Indians. Now she agreed with George; he had not seen a Gypsy, but an Indian, there in the forest. And it was very possible that he was a good man.

Early the next morning the Catlins' hired man ran in to tell the family that there were Gypsies camping on the farm. When George's father went out to see, he took George with him.

Not far from the Catlin house, a fire smoked up. A man and a woman and a little girl were sitting around the fire, and even from a distance George recognized the man he had seen in the forest. As if to prove it, a deer carcass hung suspended between two wooden poles. Mr. Catlin took one quick look and told George he had been right. These were not Gypsies, but Indians. Mr. Catlin was carrying his rifle, but he and George approached the campfire cautiously all the same.

As they came near, the little girl huddled up to her mother, but the man stood up and walked forward. He spoke English when he introduced himself as On-O-Gong-Way, of the Oneida tribe.

"I come in peace," he said.

He went on to tell them that he had lived nearby as a boy. He had hunted and fished on the Catlin farm, before it was a farm at all. But one day he and his people had been sent away. This had happened when he was very young. Still, On-O-Gong-Way had always remembered that, before he left, his father had buried an enormous pot of solid gold near an elm tree. Now he, On-O-Gong-Way, had come back to find it. His family was poor, times were hard for them, and the pot of gold could be sold to make them rich. He had walked more than a hundred and fifty miles with his wife and little girl. But now that they were here, he had not found the pot. He had already dug deep in the place he thought it ought to be, and it was not there.

Mr. Catlin thought back to the time when his land was first plowed. A little brass pot had turned up under the black soil. It was just an old-fashioned spittoon, a thing of little value, but he had kept it as a curio. That might be the pot On-O-Gong-Way was seeking. He sent the hired man back to the house to fetch it.

As soon as On-O-Gong-Way saw the pot, he recognized it. This was the treasure his father had buried for safekeeping. He looked at it long and hard, and then handed it back to Mr. Catlin.

"When I was a boy," he said sadly, "the pot of gold seemed much brighter, and larger too."

Mr. Catlin told him that the pot was not gold, but brass. He felt sorry that On-O-Gong-Way had come so far for so little, and so did George.

On-O-Gong-Way gazed off for a moment, then tightened his lips and shook his head. No one spoke. Mr. Catlin looked over at the little girl and her mother. They both looked frightened. George watched them, feeling sad and strange.

But then On-O-Gong-Way smiled tenderly at George and pointed toward the deer.

"You are a good hunter and a brave boy," he said,

and then George knew for certain that the Indian really had seen him the evening before.

That afternoon, after George and his father had returned to the house, On-O-Gong-Way came to their door, carrying a large, well-cut roast of venison. It was for George, he said, as his share of the deer. And George knew then that the feelings he had had about On-O-Gong-Way were right; the two of them could be friends.

The Indian family stayed on at the Catlin farm, and each day George visited his new friend. On-O-Gong-Way gave George a tomahawk and showed him how to throw it. George had a few arrows, and On-O-Gong-Way made a quiver for them from the deerskin. George, in turn, brought On-O-Gong-Way and his family cakes and pies from Mrs. Catlin's kitchen.

But one day, On-O-Gong-Way could teach George nothing more. The Indian was found, not far from his camp, with two bullets in his chest; his wife and little girl were gone away . . . dead or alive . . . no one knew where. The woods of Pennsylvania were once again free of Indians.

But George Catlin had made a friend he would never forget. He had come to know that an Indian could be a fine man. And he had also learned that an Indian could be a murdered man, for no reason save that he was an Indian.

*Stu-mick-O-sucks*
*A Blackfoot chief*

# chapter two

As George Catlin grew up, he continued to practice with the tomahawk that On-O-Gong-Way had given him. He taught his friends and his brother to throw it too, but none of them could throw it as straight and true as George, for no one else had learned from an Oneida hunter.

Once one of George's friends threw the tomahawk too close to George, and it left a long gash down the side of his face. He was more proud of this gash than anything else. It seemed to make him more a part of the wilderness, and of a way of life he yearned to know better. As George grew up, his best times were spent hunting and fishing and listening to the noises of the wild parts of the forest, where no cows nor plows, nor back-breaking farm work came.

George didn't want to be a farmer. He didn't want to spend his life worrying about crops, lifting loads of hay, and always wondering if there would be cash enough for a new plow when it was needed. Fortunately his father was a well-to-do farmer, with money enough to educate his sons, and he wanted to see one of them become a lawyer. So George, although he was no scholar, decided to go away and study law.

He went off to the oldest law school in America, in Litchfield, Connecticut. There he soon grew bored with sitting indoors and reading heavy, dusty law books, filled with accounts of long and tedious cases. The courtroom where he listened to cases was only a little more interesting to him. But there, at least, he could sit and scratch pictures of the judge, jury, accused and their lawyers in the wood of the courtroom bar. While he was drawing he generally closed his ears to the interminable arguments and pompous language of the court. He learned to caricature the people he watched very well. He also began to wonder, when the bar was almost covered with his pictures and he had learned nothing of the law, whether he shouldn't become an artist.

George soon became convinced that art was his real interest, so he wrote to his father and told him what he wanted to do. His father answered that a man might make his mark on the world in many ways. With his letter he sent the names and brief biographies of a few artists and suggested that George seek to learn from these men and aim as high as these masters. With this, he wished him all success in his work. Armed with his father's good wishes, and capsule biographies of Raphael, Michelangelo and Leon-

ardo da Vinci, George Catlin said good-bye to Litchfield and its law books and went to Philadelphia to
study painting.

His art-school days did not last long, however.
George was good at making people look like themselves; furthermore, he was pleasant company and
good-looking, even with the four-inch tomahawk scar
that went down his cheek. So people with money to
spend were eager to have him paint their portraits.
Before long he had set up shop as a portrait painter.
Almost at once he had as many commissions as he
could handle.

One of the people who came to have her portrait
done was a young lady from Albany, New York,
named Clara Gregory. While he was painting Clara,
Catlin fell in love with her, and after she returned
to Albany, he decided to follow her.

In Albany, George courted Clara, and also set up
a studio and began painting portraits. Before long
he found out that there were still some Indians nearby.
George had not known any Indians since On-O-Gong-
Way, but they still fascinated him. He sought some out
and asked them to sit for him. It was a pleasure for
him to paint them . . . yet he could not help but
notice how unlike On-O-Gong-Way, in all but their
appearance, these Indians were. They were not brave
hunters, and far too many of them drank too much
whiskey. Still, his interest in Indians grew, and he
began to wonder about the Indians in the far Western
Territories, where there were no cities and no farms.
There the Indians lived and hunted over a territory

of thousands of miles. What were they like? How long would they be free and strong?

Slowly an idea began to form in Catlin's mind. It was an idea that had really begun, he realized, on that day he had first met On-O-Gong-Way. He would go West and visit the people of the Great Plains, paint portraits of them. He remembered the Greek and Roman statues and artifacts he had seen in the Philadelphia Museum, and went so far as to think that he might bring back things made by the American Indians for a museum. Ever since On-O-Gong-Way had given him a tomahawk and made him a deerskin quiver, Catlin had thought that the things the Indians made were beautiful.

But it was not only the happy days with On-O-Gong-Way that he remembered. He could not forget, much as he wished he could, the sight of the Indian's strong, straight body stretched out on the bloody earth. And it was this memory that made him realize he would have to go West soon. People were saying that one day the vast Western Territories would be opened for farming and settlements; the East was becoming too crowded for the many peoples who were coming from the cities and farmlands of Europe. Remembering the fate of On-O-Gong-Way and his people when farms and towns had come to their hunting grounds, Catlin knew all too well that Indians and their culture could vanish in a very brief time. Their implements and weapons and clothes could soon be as dead and gone as a Roman in a toga, or a Greek warrior on the plains of Troy.

Just as this idea was taking hold, George's favorite brother, Julius, was drowned. There was evidence that he had been murdered while he was swimming, by someone who stole his gold watch, but nothing was ever proved. George felt that he had to go someplace where he wouldn't always be reminded of the tragedy, for Julius seemed to haunt his every thought. That meant he couldn't go back to Philadelphia, or to any place in Pennsylvania. And so, with Clara Gregory as his bride, he moved to Washington, D.C., where he set up a studio. Yet, in spite of tragedy and marriage, his dream of painting Indians did not die.

Many distinguished and famous people soon heard of Catlin and came to have their portraits painted. He made friends with people who sat for him, and through them met many other people. Some of these were in the government. He was invited to many dinner parties, where the talk was of the most important issues of the day. After dinner, the talk among the men often turned to the American Indian. People had strong opinions about what should be done with the Indian tribes, and most plans that were discussed seemed to be plans that would take away the lands the Indians still owned. A bill then in Congress proposed to take all of the Indians living in the eastern United States and move them West, whether they wanted to go or not. There they would be out of the way of the growing civilization of the white man, at least for the time being.

Many Indian tribes who still controlled their own lands were sending delegations to Washington to plead for the right to retain their lands. People who had never before set foot on a paved street, people who had never before eaten a meal that was not taken from the wilderness, were coming thousands of miles on a dangerous and uncertain journey to discuss their fate and that of their people. They were discussing this fate in a language completely unlike their own, and decisions were based, when they were at all fair, upon laws that came from Europe, that were completely unlike those the Indians used among themselves. It must have taken a great deal of courage for them to come, Catlin felt, more courage even than their great hunting and war parties required. Yet a great deal was at stake, and many Indians seemed to know that the future of their tribes, perhaps forever, was being decided in those days.

One day, as Catlin was heading for his studio, he saw a group of these Indians walking down the street. They seemed to have the same look of peace and joy on their faces that Catlin had seen On-O-Gong-Way wear the day they had met in the forest. These Indians wore robes of soft buffalo skin, bleached white and embroidered with porcupine quills. As Catlin thought about how beautiful the clothes were, and how brave the Indians appeared, it struck him that, perhaps soon, people like this would be gone forever from the earth. He made up his mind to go immediately to record them with his paintbrush before they vanished.

Once his decision was made, Catlin was determined not to wait. And Clara Catlin did nothing to stand in his way; she was not to go, but he would go with her blessing. So in 1830, paintbox in hand, he left Washington for St. Louis, Missouri. There he wanted to find a way up the great Missouri River into the bluffs and prairies of the then unorganized territory that we now know as the Dakotas, Nebraska and Wyoming. In St. Louis he hoped to have the help of a man who knew more than any other white man about the Indians of the West, William Clark. Twenty-six years earlier, he and Meriwether Lewis, at the direction of President Thomas Jefferson, had explored the Northwest, and had gone all the way to the Pacific Ocean. Clark had learned the languages of many of the peoples along the way; he had learned their customs, what they ate, what plants they used, the weather they enjoyed, and all the many things Catlin wanted to know about the land and people he was determined to see and record. With help from William Clark, Catlin felt sure his mission would succeed.

*A Konsa warrior*

# chapter three

Although he was known to be a stern and fierce old man, hard to get to know, impatient with strangers, General William Clark liked George Catlin. Clark said that the few portraits of Indians Catlin had brought along were the only good ones he had ever seen, and offered to help Catlin in his project. Like Catlin, Clark was worried about what might happen to the Indians. He felt that public opinion was so against them that it was increasingly difficult to pass any legislation on their behalf. He thought Catlin's pictures might help people to know and respect the Indian before it was too late. Clark's concern simply added to Catlin's own determination to do well what he had come to do.

Because William Clark was one of the very few white men the Indians trusted, many of them came to St. Louis to plead for justice in their struggle to hold

19

onto to their lands. Catlin was given a spot in Clark's office where he could set up his easel. There he quietly watched and painted the Indians as they spoke with their friend. They came dressed in the velvety skins of buffalo and mountain goat, soft as only a squaw knew how to make them. These clothes were richly embroidered with porcupine quills and decorated with bright bird feathers, wolf tails, and little ermine tails and paws. Around their necks the braves often wore grizzly-bear claw necklaces, as proof that they had battled with a grizzly bear and won. And along the hems of their garments hung the things that white men dreaded seeing—the scalps that the Indians had taken in battle from their enemies. Most Indian visitors had smeared their faces for the visit with red earth, giving their naturally brown skins a bright red glow. Almost all carried calumets, or peacepipes, as a sign that they came in peace. They also carried tomahawks, as a sign that they meant to keep what they believed to be theirs, by force if need be. They spoke on and on, gesturing as they spoke, first with a peacepipe, then with a tomahawk.

Catlin painted many portraits in Clark's office, but the more Indians he saw, the more he wanted to visit the western lands. He wanted to see the Indians at home and on the hunt. His determination grew, and finally one day the opportunity he had waited for came.

General Clark was going to visit a tribe of Konsa Indians who lived in the territory that is today called Kansas, and he invited Catlin to join him. The two went by boat, and after a considerable journey they were met at the riverbank by a Konsa brave. He led them silently through the tall prairie grass, where wolves lurked. Here and there a lone Indian sentinel stood. And at last the village came into view. Catlin was full of wonder and pleasure as he approached the Indian homes. It was the first time he had ever been in an Indian village. The first thing he noticed was the large number of noisy, yipping dogs, of a breed he had never seen before. Then he saw their tall, loose-limbed masters, and finally the women, carrying heavy loads on their backs. Little children peeked shyly at him, and all the Indians looked with great curiosity at the easels, paper and canvas, and wooden panels, paintbox and brushes that he carried with him. Catlin, for his part, could hardly contain himself. He wanted to begin painting at once. But there was much, much more to see, and he knew there would be time to observe and paint many things. General Clark had a great deal to talk over with the Konsas. It would be a long stay. And so, as General Clark talked, Catlin painted, and observed.

The two men remained with the Konsas until winter grew near. Then, afraid that the river might freeze and they might be unable to get back to St. Louis, they had to leave. On that return voyage, Catlin knew that his life work was decided; his job was to paint as many Indians as he could. He liked riverboat travel; he liked the wildness of the West; and he liked the Indians he had already painted. What he had done was only a beginning. He had to see and paint much, much more. He wanted to penetrate even farther into

*Wi-jun-jon aboard*
The Yellowstone

the West, and paint lands and people few white men had ever seen. Once back in the chaotic, frenzied bustle of the waterfront city of St. Louis, he already missed the clean orderliness of the Indian village and the sweet hot smell of the dust and prairie grass.

Catlin returned to Washington and to his wife, filled with the wonder and happiness of what he had found. All winter he frantically painted society portraits, so that he could leave his wife well provided for when he went back to St. Louis in the spring. He took on many more commissions than he normally would. And though he was driven by economic need, he realized he was also learning to record people's gestures and features with speed and accuracy; and he knew this ability would help him later when he was trying to paint as many Indian portraits as possible.

Spring came, and with it the longed-for trip west. When Catlin arrived at St. Louis everyone in the city was talking about a ship that was being built, a ship so well-engineered that it could navigate the swirling, fierce mud-baths of the upper Missouri River. On it fur traders could venture into a land that had formerly been extremely difficult and dangerous to reach, a land rich in furs. This was important to the people of St. Louis. Many of them had grown rich, or hoped to, by buying beaver and ermine furs from the Indians and selling them to people in such faraway places as Paris and London. The new ship was called *The Yellowstone*. Its maiden voyage was to take it up to the spot where the Missouri River joined the Yellowstone River, at the border of what is today northeastern

Montana. This was the site of the farthest fur-trading post in America at that time. A man named Pierre Chouteau, who was the grandson of the co-founder of St. Louis, René Auguste Chouteau, and himself one of the richest men in America, was building *The Yellowstone* with his own money.

George Catlin was determined, somehow, to be one of the few passengers on that maiden voyage. He would go up the river, and when he arrived in the West, he would paint as many pictures as he could of the Indians he found at the fur-trading post. Then he would make his way back to St. Louis alone on a small boat or raft. It would be a hard journey, and he would have to be back in St. Louis before the wild blizzards of winter stranded him in the wilderness. But by traveling alone, he could stop when and where he wished and paint as many of the tribes along the two thousand miles of river as he wanted.

Catlin didn't know how he was going to accomplish any of this, especially the voyage on *The Yellowstone*. But then he was commissioned to paint a portrait of one of Pierre Chouteau's children. In this way he got to know the owner of *The Yellowstone* and was invited to a number of the millionaire's dinner parties. He was even lucky enough to be seated next to the host many times.

Pierre Chouteau liked Catlin and eventually invited him to be a guest on *The Yellowstone*. Chouteau was going himself and felt it would be pleasant to have an eager but sophisticated companion who would make even the wild river seem an elegant place to be. George

Catlin, although he loved the Indians and the wilderness, was such a man.

Amid great cheering and celebration the ship finally set off. As Catlin looked around at his fellow passengers, he was astonished to see an Indian he had painted the previous year. The man's name was Wi-jun-jon, or "The Pigeon's Egg Head," and he was the son of an Assiniboin chief. Because he was a very brave warrior he had been chosen by his father and his people to speak for them before the President of the United States. The year before he had worn a beautiful soft buckskin shirt and leggings. Now as Catlin saw him again, he was dressed like a Washington dandy. Andrew Jackson, the President of the United States, had given him a suit of dark blue broadcloth, with enormous gold epaulettes on the shoulders. Wi-jun-jon's naturally graceful sloping shoulders were padded ridiculously high; he could scarcely walk in the high polished boots he wore, and his neck was held so stiff by the collar of the suit that he could not comfortably turn his head. He wore a tall beaver hat with a bright red feather; on his hands were white kid dancing gloves, imported from France; in one hand he carried an umbrella, although it was not raining; and in the other hand he carried a silk fan painted with pretty little scenes.

Catlin painted Wi-jun-jon's portrait again, and as he sat for the portrait, the Indian often took long drinks from a gallon jug of whiskey that accompanied him at all times. He talked to Catlin of nothing but the gay and beautiful social life of the Washington ballrooms, and the lovely ladies who had chattered with him from behind their fans as they danced beneath tinkling chandeliers. Catlin was dismayed at what a year of the white man's society had done to a fine Indian.

When *The Yellowstone* entered the rapids of the upper Missouri, Catlin saw, for the first time, great herds of buffalo. They blackened the bluffs as they galloped through the tall buffalo grass. Catlin had never seen animals in such vast quantities.

Soon the steamboat entered the country of the Poncas and other remote Indian tribes. There Catlin watched, horrified, from the decks of the steamboat, as whole villages of Indians ran screaming in panic at the sound of *The Yellowstone's* steam whistle. Brave warriors, who had chased unafraid among the buffalo and fought alone with grizzly bears, ran in terror at the unknown sound. But *The Yellowstone* moved on, whistling as it went, carrying fur traders, coops of live chickens, food of all sorts, whiskey and guns, little glass beads to trade for furs, George Catlin and his paint-box, and Wi-jun-jon.

At last *The Yellowstone* reached its first stop, Fort Pierre, named after Pierre Chouteau, in what is today South Dakota. Here Pierre Chouteau wished to visit and talk with the Blackfeet and Sioux. They had more furs to trade than any other Indians. Chouteau was going to march over the plains with a party of about twenty men to a spot where a Sioux encampment stood, and he invited Catlin to go along. The men walked for nearly a week, and then one day stood and looked down from a bluff; there before them, spread out on a plain were more than six hundred tepees of the handsome and warlike Sioux.

As soon as the greetings were over, Catlin asked to paint the chief, Ha-won-je-tah, or "The One Horn." He was called this because of a mysterious little horn he always wore around his neck. He was a tall, strong man with long black hair. His strength and courage were already legendary; people said he could run as fast on foot as a buffalo and stab it with his arrow straight to the heart. Catlin took out his paintbrushes and paintbox and folding easel, and with great joy, began to paint Ha-won-je-tah. It was a moment of triumph for him. He had come twelve hundred miles from St. Louis just for this.

No one had ever painted a picture of a Sioux chief in his own tepee before. As Catlin sat painting, some of the braves of the tribe crept softly in, and one by one they clapped their hands silently over their open mouths. This was an Indian's way of expressing wonder and amazement; Catlin had seen the gesture before. When the portrait was done, word spread throughout the encampment of the wonderful picture of Ha-won-je-tah that the white man had painted. Catlin was given a name of great honor. He was called Ee-cha-soo-ka-wa-kon, which meant "The Medicine Painter." "Medicine" was the word the French traders had originally given to the various mysteries and magical rites the Indians performed, and to the Sioux, Catlin's paintings appeared truly magical.

But not everyone approved of the painting. Some of

the medicine men of the tribe said that their chief would never again sleep at night, for after all, his eyes in the picture could never be shut. The squaws began to cry. The braves who had so admired the painting turned their heads in the opposite direction whenever Catlin looked at them, afraid that he might capture their likeness on canvas, too, and that they like the chief might never again sleep at night. But Ha-won-je-tah was as interested in new things as the women and medicine men were conservative, and he assured his people that he was not at all afraid of encountering any bad effects from having his portrait painted. After that many of the handsome Sioux braves asked to have their portraits painted, and Catlin had as many models as he could have wished. He kept many of his portraits, but perhaps he painted duplicates, for he gave each man who sat for him a picture he could keep. The braves carried their pictures around with them and took excellent care of them, for they were convinced that if harm came to the portrait, it would also come to the man himself.

Finally Chouteau's party hiked the long way back to Fort Pierre, and the steamboat began to move on, toward Fort Union, eight hundred miles up the river. There, at the end of the journey, Wi-jun-jon would return to his people, and George Catlin would begin his leisurely trip back down the two thousand miles of river.

The eight hundred miles were covered, but not all of the party were as eager to leave the ship as Catlin. Wi-jun-jon stepped off the boat a sadder sight than when he had boarded at St. Louis. The whiskey jug and three months of sleeping in his clothes had not done much for his elegant outfit: the white kid gloves were black with dirt; the pretty fan was broken and its silk was torn; the umbrella was ripped, the beaver hat was crushed. Catlin watched sadly as the Assiniboin brave greeted his wife. At first neither she, nor the other Indians meeting him, recognized him. But slowly their hands went up before their open mouths, and Wi-jun-jon began to tell them of his wonderful adventure. He had come home.

*Ha-won-je-tah*
*A Sioux chief*

# chapter four

At Fort Union, Catlin met two men who also wanted to take a small boat downriver to St. Louis. The three of them decided to make the journey together. The two men were French fur trappers, Baptiste and Bogarde. They were accustomed to the wilderness, and Catlin knew that his journey would be safer with them. They had no objection to his plan of stopping to paint portraits of the Indians, because they intended to obtain furs from the same Indians.

The three men equipped a small skiff with the things they needed: dried buffalo tongues and beaver tails to eat, a little sugar and plenty of coffee, a coffeepot and a frying pan. There were also beaver furs that Baptiste and Bogarde planned to sell in St. Louis, Catlin's folding easel and paintbox, and the paintings he had made along the way. Somewhere on his journey Catlin had also acquired a pet, a tame war eagle,

31

and that came, too. Baptiste and Bogarde built a perch for him in the bow of the skiff.

Before leaving Fort Union, Catlin was saddened by a final word about Wi-jun-jon. The Assiniboins had soon grown tired of his boasting about the things he had seen and done in Washington, and one of them had called him a liar. Wi-jun-jon reacted by hitting the man, and a fight broke out. More than a year of soft living and hard drinking had left Wi-jun-jon less of a warrior than he had been when Catlin had first met him in General Clark's office in St. Louis. He was killed in the fight.

With Catlin feeling all the more impatient to set about his work after word of Wi-jun-jon's death, the three men set out one morning, for their long trip down the Missouri River. The first visit they made was to the Crow and Blackfoot Indians. These people were reputed to be as brave and fierce as the Sioux. Catlin, however, found them to be polite, peaceful and welcoming. Among other things, they taught him to hunt buffalo. They showed him that although a buffalo would charge in panic at sight of a man, a wolf could move easily among the black herds. Therefore a man could sneak up on the buffalo if he was dressed in a wolf skin. Catlin tried it and discovered that he could sketch the grazing buffalo from very close. He did this often, because he was gradually growing as curious about the great beasts of the prairie as he was about the people who lived by hunting them. As he sketched he could smell the hot breath of the buffalo as they chomped the tall buffalo grass, and instead of being afraid, Catlin was elated. This was the life he loved. Catlin made many paintings of the tall and magnificient Crow warriors. They never cut their hair, and it often grew to be as much as ten feet long; it trailed after them freely as they strolled through their villages. They washed it often in the river, and each day they rubbed it with buffalo fat so that it was always black and shiny. As they galloped across the prairie on horseback, their hair blew in the wind and shone like a long, black river as the sun struck it. A feeling of movement, quick as water, was the impression Catlin got of the Crow warriors as they raced across the prairies on their ponies. Catlin tried to capture this impression of color and motion in his paintings. To him it seemed an ideal union of men with the wilderness. Though they had not had horses before the Spanish brought them, once they had learned to ride, the Plains Indians had changed from semisedentary food gatherers into far-ranging hunters on horseback. Their entire way of life was based upon the horse, the buffalo, and constant motion, with collapsible, portable, tall tepees of buffalo hide for their homes. It was a way of life Catlin envied.

While Catlin painted the Indians and their buffalo, he wondered constantly what was to become of these people as the white man moved west. He thought of Wi-jun-jon, and he thought back to his old friend On-O-Gong-Way, now long dead. He felt strongly that the Indian way of life should not disappear; and he decided that the only way it could be preserved was to make the entire upper Missouri and Yellowstone region into a vast Indian hunting ground. He saw it as a sort of huge park, without roads, farms, or villages . . . nothing in fact, that was not there already. At that time there were no national parks or wilderness areas set aside in America. The vastness of America seemed to most people to be without limit, and there seemed to be enough land for all. But the way of life of the Plains Indian was dependent on the buffalo and on greater open spaces than any people of European descent had ever known. The Indians needed a vast park, and Catlin hoped that if ever such a park came to be, people would remember that he, George Catlin, had first thought of it. He wondered to himself how such a plan could be brought to reality.

More and more, as he traveled and searched for a way to make Indian life real to white people, Catlin felt that he needed more of Indian culture to display than just the paintings he had made. He wanted other people to see the beautiful things the Indians made. So he began to collect tepees, tomahawks, peacepipes, leggings, war bonnets, and many other things, made by hand with a careful and loving craftsmanship that was beginning to disappear in the world Catlin came from. There was one item he was especially eager to buy, for it told more about the Indians and their religion than anything else, but he could not persuade anyone to sell him one. And no wonder, for it was a medicine bag.

Each Indian man, among all the tribes Catlin came to know, carried with him his medicine bag. When he was between twelve and fourteen years old, an Indian

*The Bear Dance of the Sioux*

boy was sent out into the wilderness to discover his own "medicine." For a long time he sat alone and thought and watched the sun and the moon and the tall grass. Then at last, he fell asleep and dreamed. The first animal or stone or plant he dreamed of was his "medicine," and he had to find it and bring it or some part of it home. If he dreamed of a grouse, a grouse feather might be his medicine. If he dreamed a strange dream, of a creature he did not recognize, an unusual fossil might be his medicine. If he dreamed of a wolf, a few hairs from a wolf's coat, or a sharp wolf tooth could be his medicine. When the boy returned, still alone, to his village, with the medicine he had dreamed of, searched for, and found, it was placed by a medicine man in a beautiful soft leather pouch, and sealed permanently. In this way, during a time of aloneness, a boy learned about himself and acquired a sign that would guide him throughout his life. He also, it was believed, formed a mysterious but unbreakable union with the natural world through his medicine. Therefore, no Indian would part with his medicine bag; it was the clue to the deepest part of his soul. Even when an Indian died, his medicine bag accompanied his body. If a medicine bag was taken from a man in battle, he was treated as if he had died; and often he did, for his very soul had disappeared with the little bag that was filled with so much mystery. With the ever-growing respect and admiration Catlin felt for the Indians, he was not surprised to discover among them such deep and genuine religious feeling. And he respected it.

The time came for Catlin, Baptiste and Bogarde to move on down the river to the next Indian settlement, if St. Louis were to be reached before winter came. Baptiste and Bogarde talked almost constantly of the wealth that would come to them when they sold their furs in the city, and of the good times they would have in the saloons and dance halls of St. Louis when they got there. Catlin, for his part, wrote down memories of the trip, for it was the adventures he was having on the river, not those that he might have in the city, that appealed to him.

*Sah-ko-Kah*
*A young Mandan woman*

# chapter five

Catlin waited with unconcealed impatience for the next Indians they were to meet, the Mandans. General Clark had told him of these people who lived along the banks of the Missouri and who were quite different in appearance, language and customs from their neighbors. They were a polite and friendly people, and Clark had come to love them and value their friendship above all other Indians'. Catlin had spent long hours hearing about them, the People of the Pheasant, and he wanted to know them himself.

As the skiff moved along down the river, the three men had to camp on shore at night. Their boat was so laden with tepees, furs, paintings, and many other treasures, that there was no room aboard to sleep. One morning Catlin was preparing breakfast for the three of them before the other two awoke. The coffeepot was boiling on the fire when he saw, not far off, a lone buffalo cow. Thinking of what a supper she would make, fresh meat cooked on an open fire, Catlin left the campfire and set out after her. But the buffalo sensed his nearness and ran off before he could shoot. When he returned to the fire, where the precious coffee-pot had stood, a scorched and melted chunk of tin lay, and the breakfast coffee had long ago sizzled away on the hot rocks. To Bogarde and Catlin it seemed a small enough loss, but not to Baptiste. He was miserable without his coffee, not fit to live with. Catlin tried to cook coffee in the frying pan, but it tasted strongly of buffalo fat, and Baptiste could not drink it. Finally, in desperation, the fur trader tried a taste of raw coffee mixed with a little sugar, and as he licked it off his rough hands, joy spread across his face. The rest of the way down the river, Baptiste took his coffee raw.

There were other experiences in camp. One night the men were awakened by a strange noise. Catlin peered out and saw a large grizzly bear nosing among their supplies. Remembering that Baptiste could not do without his coffee, Catlin shouted, and the bear ran away. The coffee was safe, as was the sugar, but unfortunately, the bear had tasted Catlin's paints, which were packed in little tubes made from pig's bladders. Some of his colors were gone. Although his range of colors was now a bit limited, fortunately enough paints were salvaged so that Catlin could go on with his work. The three men set off at once in the night, however; for the river, swift and dark as it was, seemed more welcoming than the land.

At last they reached the Mandan village. The Mandans did not live in tepees, for they were not among the nomadic Plains Indians. Their homes were great domed structures, made of clay and wattle, with narrow little pathways between them. Catlin had never before seen buildings like the Mandan lodges, and they fascinated him. As he entered the village, he could see many people sitting up on the big domes, sunbathing, and watching him with curiosity. One of the first friends he made among the Mandans was their second chief, Ma-to-toh-pa, or "The Four Bears." This chief immediately agreed to let Catlin paint his portrait.

When the portrait was nearly done, a young brave entered Ma-to-toh-pa's lodge and glanced at the painting. He turned his head quickly aside, for no one who respected a chief ever looked him straight in the eye; and to the Indian, Catlin's painting was surely the chief. Like the Sioux, the Mandans thought Catlin was a man of much mystery and magic, for Indians did not do realistic and representational painting. What Catlin did was completely unknown among them. Catlin was amused by this and tried to explain to the Mandans that his art was something many people could learn, if they were taught. No one among the Indians believed him.

Each Mandan brave soon wanted to be painted, and Catlin had many splendid-looking models. In fact, he had so many willing sitters that he had to paint more rapidly than ever before; there were many days when he painted portraits of six braves between sunrise and sunset. At last a great honor was bestowed upon him by Ma-to-toh-pa. He was given a medicine man's rattle, called a *she-she-quoi*. It was decorated with such items as grizzly-bear claws, wings of bats, and ermine skins; and it was well rubbed with skunk musk, which gave the rattle a pungent smell. Catlin felt he had been done a great honor and had been given a wonderful treasure. He was proud to have the rattle in his collection.

During the time he had spent in the Mandan village, as well as in other Indian villages, Catlin had noticed certain men, who were magnificently dressed, better dressed than any warriors. These men did not go off to hunt when the other men did. They stayed in the village and played ball with the young children, talked with the squaws, and sunbathed. Catlin asked one of these men if he would pose for him, for his outfit was especially beautiful, and the young man gladly agreed to do so. But when Catlin showed the finished portrait to the chief, Ma-to-toh-pa was angry. He explained to Catlin that this was a man who had failed at least one of the many tests of endurance and courage that were given to young boys to be sure they were brave and agile and strong enough for the dangerous life of hunting and fighting that was ahead for them. Those who failed never acquired the status of braves, but instead remained as children and were considered good enough only to stay in villages and amuse the children and talk with the women. They were fed and clothed well, treated well, and were liked by the women and children. But the braves did not associate with

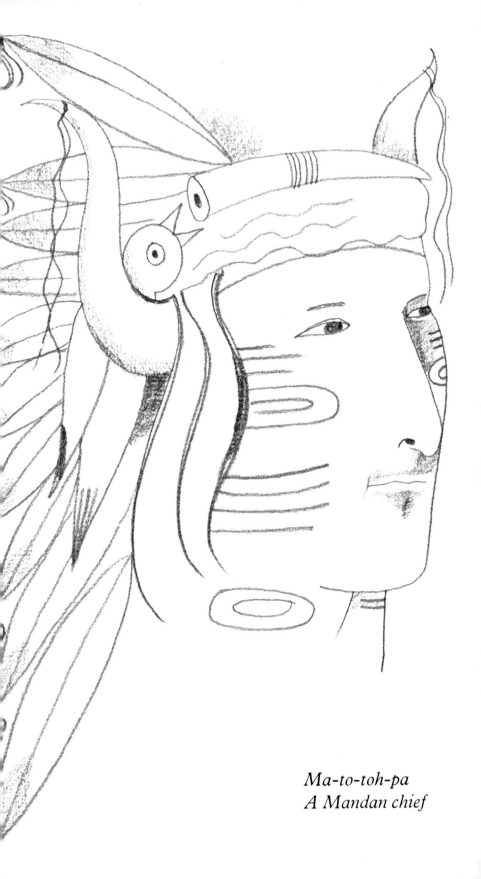

*Ma-to-toh-pa*
*A Mandan chief*

them; it would be, the chief explained, a serious insult to the braves Catlin had painted for the artist to also honor this man, a proven coward, with a portrait. So, reluctantly, for he liked the picture, Catlin destroyed it.

Not everyone was happy with Catlin's presence in the Mandan village, however. One man especially hated him. This man sat outside Catlin's studio and kept up a grim chant, listing all of the terrible things that would befall those Mandans who allowed the white man to steal their likenesses. This man was Mah-to-he-ha, or "The Old Bear." He was head medicine man of the tribe. Since he seemed to have a great deal of influence over the women, Catlin was afraid they would turn their husbands against having their portraits painted. He had been very fortunate, he felt, in having been accepted and welcomed. But there was always the chance that one day he would no longer be wanted, and not only his work, but perhaps even his life, would be in danger. So he searched long and hard for a way to change Mah-to-he-ha's strong prejudice against him.

One day, as Mah-to-he-ha sat wailing by the door, Catlin began to talk to him. Mah-to-he-ha, Catlin said, was a most distinguished looking man. In fact, Catlin went on, he had only been practicing when he did portraits of the other Mandans, to make certain he was skilled enough to paint so noble, handsome and important a person as Mah-to-he-ha. Not, Catlin finished, that he ever expected to be so fortunate as to have this opportunity, but he wanted to be ready, just the same. Mah-to-he-ha surprised even Catlin (although he had suspected that the medicine man was quite vain) by how quickly he stopped his cursing song. He shook Catlin's hand and suggested they smoke the peacepipe together.

Next Mah-to-he-ha ordered the women to prepare a steam bath for him. The women gathered hot stones from a fire and set them under a large wicker basket that was constructed just for this purpose. It was placed in a tent just outside the domed village. The women put herbs and roots on the hot stones and when Mah-to-he-ha entered the tent, he sat in the wicker basket and the women poured hot water over the heated stones. Aromatic vapors surrounded Mah-to-he-ha and he came out glowingly clean and relaxed. Then he plunged into the chill water of the river, to close his pores. After this he smeared his face with bright-colored clays, tied foxtails to his legs, and put on a sort of apron of a boar's head. All ready then, he came to Catlin, who sat eagerly waiting at his easel. The painting began, and Mah-to-he-ha sang a magical medicine song throughout the sitting. The atmosphere created by the medicine man in his ceremonial dress singing his eerie song must have been just what Catlin needed to make his triumph complete; for when the portrait was done, Mah-to-he-ha pronounced it the finest thing he had ever seen. Catlin often saw him after that stretched out full length on the ground, gazing at his portrait with wonder and admiration. He became one of Catlin's closest friends, and through this friendship Catlin heard many of the tales the Mandans

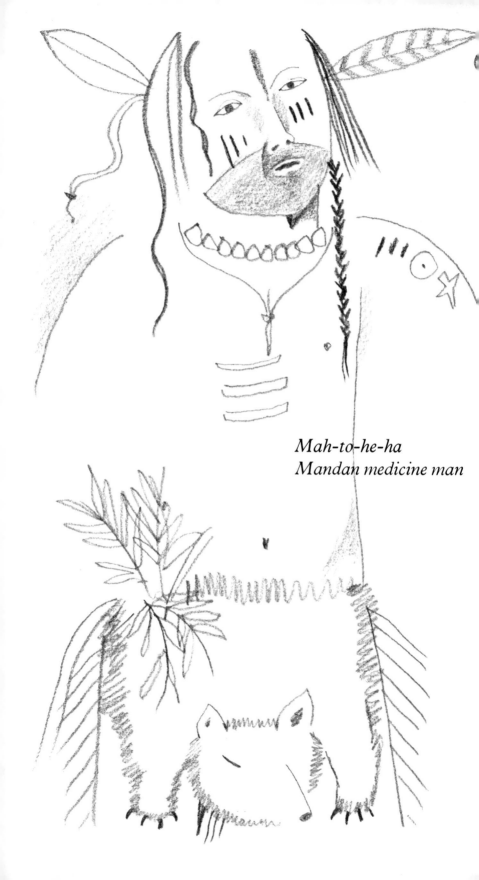

*Mah-to-he-ha*
*Mandan medicine man*

told and witnessed many secret ceremonies that few, if any, outsiders had ever seen. He was even able to paint pictures of some of them.

In the Mandan village Catlin began to wonder where the American Indians had come from. In Catlin's time nothing was known of prehistory and the movements of early men. Even today, no one knows for certain from where or when the American Indians reached this continent; but at the sight of the Mandans, Catlin became exceedingly curious. Today, from what is known of their language, the Mandan tongue seems to have been one of the Sioux family of languages. But in many ways the Mandans were very different from other Indians. They did not look like other Indians. They were often blue-eyed. Many of them had brown instead of blue-black hair. Others had the strangest hair Catlin had ever seen. These were the Mandans that French fur traders called *chevaux gris*. Their hair was a beautiful shade of pearl gray, nearly white. The people who had hair this color had not acquired it with years, but were born with it. It was not at all unusual to see tiny gray-haired children running and laughing around the narrow alleys of the Mandan village.

As Catlin watched some of their secret ceremonies and heard their legends, his curiosity increased. Most of the Mandan religion centered around a tale of a great flood, during which they had sought the top of a high mountain for safety. Their greatest festival was a strange, mystical, and frightening celebration of deliverance from the flood, called *O-kee-pa*. Catlin

47

made a series of paintings of this ceremony, for it fascinated him and reminded him of the Bible story of Noah. He could not help but wonder if the Mandans were not telling of a survival from the same flood.

Although the *O-kee-pa* ceremony was one of the most frightening and disturbing religious rituals that has ever been recorded, involving terrifying human torture for those young men who aspired to be braves and hunters, the Mandans themselves were in all other respects perhaps the gentlest people Catlin had ever known. They were as brave as any Plains Indians in the buffalo hunt; they defended themselves bravely if attacked; but they never made war on other people. Their chiefs always tried to follow a way of peace. The Mandans told in legend why this was so. They said that once there had been many, many Mandans, and they had lived all over the world. But they had fought constantly among themselves, until only one tribe of Mandans was left in the world. They were the last of their kind. They did not want to destroy themselves in war, and so their chosen way was peace.

One night chief Ma-to-toh-pa invited Catlin to his lodge for dinner. This lodge was like all Mandan lodges, a great domed building, about sixty feet in diameter; many members of the chief's family lived there. Ma-to-toh-pa proved to be the most gracious host Catlin had ever known, though he had dined very elegantly many times in Washington. Catlin decided as he ate that the Mandans must be a very ancient people, to have developed table manners as perfect as theirs were and dining customs as delightful. The food was delicious and beautifully served. There was pemmican, a sort of bread made from dried buffalo meat. Next to the pemmican was a dish of bright yellow buffalo fat, which was spread on the pemmican to make something much like bread and butter. There were boiled buffalo ribs, with delicious soup made from the broth in which they had been cooked. The meat and soup course was accompanied by tasty pudding made of wild currants and buffalo-berries, a fruit much like a currant, which the Mandan women gathered on the prairies. All of the food was served in gracefully carved wooden dishes, as smooth as china. The dishes were placed on a sort of tablecloth of delicately woven rush, set upon the clay floor, which although unfired, was burnished and swept until it shone as bright as marble.

Because he was a chief, Ma-to-toh-pa did not himself eat while Catlin did, but kept his guest company by telling wonderful tales of adventures he had had on the hunt. After dinner, Ma-to-toh-pa took out a pouch filled with willow-tree bark, neatly cut into tiny shavings. The bark and branches of the willow trees, which grew along the Missouri, were sacred to the Mandans, for they said that a branch of willow carried by a dove had first told them that the great flood had ended. The *O-kee-pa* ceremony began when the willow trees were in full leaf. Ma-to-toh-pa filled a pipe with the sacred bark, called *knick-kneck,* and offered it to Catlin. Then he filled his own, and the two men sat with the gentle smoke of their pipes floating up to the smoke hole in the center of the great domed ceiling, and talked quietly. Catlin could not help remembering On-O-Gong-Way smoking his pipe years before in the Pennsylvania woods. His gentleness, his look of peace, his kindness toward the boy who lay hidden there, all came back. And with this came the memory that always accompanied the first, that of On-O-Gong-Way lying dead with two bullets in his chest. The Mandans, Sioux, Blackfoot, Assiniboins and Crows . . . what would become of them?

All too soon it became apparent that the winter winds were about to blow on the prairie. Unless they planned to stay the winter, sealed in with the Mandans on the Great Plains, the three men would have to go. So one morning, Catlin, Baptiste, and Bogarde set off in their skiff. Just as they were leaving, a young brave whom Catlin had once painted tossed out a package. It was tied with many difficult knots, and the skiff was far from the many-domed Mandan village before Catlin had managed to undo them all. The package contained a pair of beautiful white leggings, made from snowy elkskins. Catlin recognized them, for he had offered to buy them, for any price. But the man would never sell them. They were the finest pants he owned and no price was high enough to make him part with them. But what was too good to sell he had given his friend as a farewell gift.

As they rode down the river toward St. Louis, Catlin was already planning to return to the Mandan village the following spring. The more he saw of these and other Indians, the more he respected them and the

*O-kee-he-de*
*The Evil Spirit dancer*
*of the Mandan* O-kee-pa *ceremony*

more he wanted to know about them.

As autumn went on, Catlin and his companions floated down the Missouri, watching the wild birds and the great black herds of buffalo. It was a peaceful, pleasant life, but one day, Baptiste and Bogarde grew quiet and apprehensive. They explained to Catlin that they were nearing the village of the Arikaras. Catlin wanted to stop and meet them, but Baptiste and Bogarde would not hear of it. They told Catlin that the Arikaras had vowed to scalp, torture and kill any white man caught entering their territory. Catlan was confused. General Clark had described the same Arikaras as a friendly people; but Baptiste and Bogarde insisted that the Arikaras had changed. The two men disguised the boat with green branches, covering it over so that it looked like a small island of floating turf. And then they set out by night to slip silently through the river. Before long they heard drumbeats and singing. Soon, by the light of a full moon, they watched Arikara braves dance around the scalps of two white fur traders they had just killed. Suddenly a group of women, swimming in the moonlit river, sighted the little boat and called out. Without waiting to see if their fate would be the same as that of the two traders, Catlin, Baptiste, and Bogarde, paddled furiously. They went on all night, until they were far from the Arikara village. Catlin could not help wondering, even as his arms ached from paddling and his heart beat fast, what had happened to change these people. Why had a tribe that had welcomed Lewis and Clark and shared with them their lore of the land, become a people who would never again look at a white face in peace and friendship? Just before winter the three men reached St. Louis, with its great docks and warehouses at the river's edge, all labeled "Chouteau." The saloons rang with piano music; ladies in hoop skirts and gentlemen in top hats mixed with fur traders in dirty deerskin jackets. Baptiste and Bogarde were jubilant. Here was the great marketplace for their furs; here were riches, and fun and all the coffee Baptiste could drink. As for Catlin, he intended to head for home, and his wife.

The skiff was well loaded with furs and paintings and the Indian articles Catlin had accumulated. They left the furs with a dealer. Then Baptiste and Bogarde helped Catlin carry his things to a cheap hotel on the waterfront. But there was too much for them to carry in one trip. They left several things behind, and in a few minutes returned. But they were too late; the skiff and the items left it it were gone. In all their journeys through Indian lands, the three had never even considered the possibility that their boat and possessions might be stolen. But back in civilization, things were not as safe. With this, the three men said goodbye and went their separate ways.

*Choctaw ball-player*

# chapter six

Catlin did not stay in St. Louis long. He stored his Indian collection in a warehouse there and went to Utica, New York, where he and Clara had decided to settle so she could be near her family. But he was not content at home. He had become so involved with the Indian people that he was happy only when he was among them. He could not bear to listen to people talking endlessly of their business affairs and money matters and the value of property, when he had so recently known the wild, fierce gaiety of the buffalo chase, and the relaxed, carefree, playful life of Indians at home. He longed for hours spent in exciting arrow-shooting contests, and for gambling games with all the laughter that accompanied them. And so he had to leave.

He did not go to see the Mandans again the following spring. Instead, his passion to know Indians, to paint them, to learn their ways, drove him farther and farther from home, and for longer and longer periods of time. He went South to the Oklahoma Territory; he went down the Mississippi River. He painted the people of many tribes, among them the Comanches, who were said to be the greatest horsemen in the world. The Comanches were physically quite different from the tall, handsome Plains Indians. The Comanches were short and squat and not at all athletic-looking or graceful when they were on the ground; but once they mounted horses, they became like the wind itself, so effortlessly did they ride. Catlin painted the Pawnees and Choctaws, playing at the ball games that they and all Indians seemed to enjoy. And while he painted he bought more and more clothing and other Indian artifacts. He also asked Indian agents and fur traders to ship any items that they could purchase to his warehouse in St. Louis.

At last, after a number of years, the warehouse contained eight tons of Indian goods: tepees, saddles, peacepipes, war bonnets, dishes, bridles, tomahawks, arrows, knives, clothing of all sorts, and many other things. Finally, Catlin hired a freight car and moved the collection to Utica. The time had come to put on an exhibition for the public, one that might help other people know the Indian as Catlin himself did. He hoped to stir up public opinion and make people realize that the Indians were not savages, but cultured human beings. If people came to know that, Catlin felt, they might force Congress to keep the Indians from being destroyed while there was still time. Clara was not happy about the things Catlin was doing. He painted less and less; his concern for the Indian seemed to have become an unreal obsession; she was afraid of where it would lead. But all the same, Catlin rented an unused church in Buffalo, New York, and ran advertisements in the papers, telling people about the show he had set up there. The exhibit was a great success; the church was always full of sightseers, for no one had ever seen anything like the things Catlin displayed. The paintings were admired; the Indian artifacts were considered most unusual and curious; and everyone in Buffalo felt that George Catlin's marvelous show was better than any other entertainment that had recently come to town.

Along with the tepees and war bonnets, and hundreds of other items on display, Catlin had a great collection of peacepipes. Although they were carved and decorated in different ways, depending upon which of the many tribes they had come from, people noticed that they were always of the same red stone. Many people asked Catlin about this stone, for it did not look like any other they had seen. Catlin knew nothing about the stone itself, but he knew from Indian medicine men that it was called the peacepipe stone, and he knew that it all came from one place, somewhere in Wisconsin. He decided to find out more about it when the exhibit closed.

As soon as the Buffalo exhibit was over, and the collection had been placed in a local warehouse, Catlin and a friend, an Englishman named Robert Wood, set out by steamboat for Wisconsin. They crossed the Great Lakes, from Utica, New York, to Green Bay,

Wisconsin, and there Catlin persuaded an Indian to take him to the peacepipe quarry.

The three men were only part way to the quarry when a group of angry Indians met them and threatened to stop them by force if they went any farther. The leader of these men said that a white man had once gone to the sacred quarry, taken a piece of the stone, and carved it into a crude, ugly, soap dish. The peacepipe-stone dish sat around, unwashed, with a lot of other dirty dishes. Such an act was a sacrilege, and these Indians did not intend to allow it to happen again. Catlin tried to explain that he had come in peace and friendship and would not misuse or harm the sacred stone. But the Indians would not believe him. They knew from experience that the word of a white man was seldom kept. Yet, for some reason, the Indians did allow Catlin and his party to continue, unharmed.

At last the three men reached the sacred place. It was a cliff of shining rock, about two miles long. All through it ran veins of red rock, which had been quarried in many places. This red rock was the pipestone. A sense of mystery seemed to surround the place. Even the air hung strange and silent over the glassy cliff, and upon the surface of the cliff wall many strange and incomprehensible pictures had been scratched. As Catlin looked at the source of the red pipestone, he remembered a story he had heard from a Sioux medicine man of how pipestone had come to the Indian people.

Once there had been nothing but war, and all Indians had hated and killed each other. There was no peace anywhere, and the Spirit that was the most powerful, that ruled over all things, grew angry. He told the medicine men of every tribe to bring his people to a certain place, for he wished to talk to them. This place was far from where any man lived. It was the home of the Thunderbird, the great she-eagle who, with her husband, the Sky-Serpent, ruled the sky. No one could live in the place where the people came, for when the two eggs that the Thunderbird laid hatched out, thunder broke the sky and the Sky-Serpent, lightning-bright, danced with joy; the noise then was so loud that no man could bear it. It was a place filled with wonder and terror. And so, those tribes who were summoned there by the Great Spirit were the first people to stand beneath the Thunderbird's nest. It was difficult to gather them there, for they fought and killed each other along the way, and although many had begun the journey, few arrived. For those that did come, amid the noise that broke the sky, the Great Spirit spoke. And he took from the mountain where the Thunderbird sat a piece of red stone with a hole in it, red the color of an Indian's skin. He blew sweet-smelling smoke from his mouth through the hole, and at that moment there was no fighting. In this way he showed all the people how to smoke the pipe of peace. He told them that they must make pipes for themselves from this stone, and only this stone, for it was theirs; he had given it to them, and it was the color of their own flesh. It was as soft when first quarried as a new-born baby's flesh; it was easy to carve then. But it hardened when finished and became as strong as a warrior's arm. The Great Spirit told the people that no weapons must ever be brought to the pipestone quarry; the stone must only be used for making peacepipes; all those who came must come in peace, and no treaty made by the smoke of the peacepipe could ever be broken, or the Great Spirit would be angry. The people who heard obeyed him, and ever after Indians smoked the peacepipe together.

From all over the North American continent, for unknown numbers of centuries, Indian medicine men of many tribes had come to take the precious stone for their peacepipes, for it was not found elsewhere. This strange stone was a bond between peoples of many different languages and cultures. Catlin, when he saw it, decided he had never seen a stone like it. So he sent a tiny piece to a minerologist at Harvard University to see if it could be classified. Later the scientist reported that he was also unable to classify the stone; it was not like any other that he knew. Therefore, he wrote, he had called it "catlinite," after the man who had first sent it in for scientific analysis. And "catlinite" is what it is called today.

On the way home from the pipestone quarry, Catlin and Robert Wood talked of Catlin's exhibit. Catlin hoped the United States government would buy his entire collection, both his paintings and his Indian artifacts, and place the things in a museum where they could be seen and studied by many people. Catlin was convinced that to know the Indian was to love and admire him, and that a permanent exhibit dedicated to the Indian would be a good way to assure the Indians of a chance to follow their own way of life. To help achieve his goal, and make people aware of what he had, Catlin decided to open an exhibit in New York City.

The New York exhibit was even more popular than the one in Buffalo had been. Catlin included a talk about the Indians he had known, but people did not like the talk as much as the objects and pictures he showed. Many people did not believe Catlin when he told them of the things he had seen; some said he was a fake and a fraud. They doubted that the Indians had been polite and courteous to him, for few believed that Indians were more than savages. When Catlin told how clean the Indians were, how bright and neat their clothes and household things were kept, many of the women in the audience snickered; they believed that Indians were always dirty and untidy. Sportsmen doubted that an Indian could shoot an arrow through a buffalo and have it come out the other side, although they seemed quite willing to believe any stories of atrocities Indians had committed against settlers.

Above all, no one seemed to want to hear what Catlin most wanted to say. He talked about white traders who brought whiskey and disease to the Indians, though many chiefs had begged them not to trade whiskey for furs. He told of having seen the United States government cheat the Indians by buying land for far less than it was worth. Worst of all, the government often did not honor treaties made by the

*Buffalo hunting*

smoke of the peacepipe; the terms were forgotten whenever it was convenient and profitable to do so. Perhaps, under the circumstances, it was not surprising that the United States government was reluctant to buy Catlin's collection. For he spoke out against government policy, not only in New York, but in Washington, Philadelphia and Boston as well. These were the cities where the most influential people in America lived; here the most powerful newspapers in the country were published. Catlin did not stop with speeches and exhibitions. He went to dinner parties with congressmen and other powerful men, and over and over he begged them to put through legislation that would save the Indians before it was too late. Save the buffaloes, too, he pleaded, for he saw that they would disappear if their grazing lands were turned into farms.

Many newspapers used their editorial pages to try to pursuade Congress to buy the Catlin collection for a museum; they saw that it was a very important part of the history of the country. The famous orator, Daniel Webster, thundered in Congress. The policy of the treatment of the Indian must be changed, he shouted. There must be justice.

Nothing worked. The collection remained unbought, and there was no new legislation. But Catlin did not give up. He simply tried a new tactic. He decided to shame Congress into buying the collection! He announced that he would no longer show his exhibit in America; he would instead take it to England and let the English have it. He was very sure that Americans would not want a foreign power, especially England, to own the collection. But he was mistaken. No offer came from Congress.

Even while important newspapers were publishing angry editorials denouncing the departure of the collection as a national shame, Catlin was packing. He and Clara now had a little girl and were soon expecting a second child. Clara would not be able to travel until after the baby was born. But Catlin felt he could not wait much longer, if his plan was to work at all. He had to take a positive step while he was still in the news. So he sent his wife and child home to her parents. And he, along with eight tons of Indian artifacts, his paintings, and two caged grizzly bears, boarded a ship for Liverpool, England.

*Mandan Buffalo dancer*

# chapter seven

It was 1839 when Catlin decided to go to England, and time seemed to be running out for the Indians. Just before he left, Catlin heard dreadful news about the Mandan Indians, among whom he had spent such pleasant days. A fur trader who was ill had gone into the Mandan village. There he had been made comfortable; he had recovered and left. But he had been ill of smallpox. Centuries of the disease had given many people of European descent some immunity. But no Mandan, or any Indian, had any immunity. Smallpox was non-existent among the American Indians before the white man came. When Catlin had visited them, eight years earlier, the Mandans had been a small tribe of no more than two thousand persons. Within a few months of the coming of the smallpox, they had all perished. The polite and friendly Mandans, the People of the Pheasant, were dead.

Where had they come from? What was their history? These questions would never be answered, for the Mandans were gone forever.

Like so many events before, this new tragedy spurred Catlin on, although just why he thought a trip to England would be useful is not wholly clear. He seemed to be driven by an idea that had no very sure meaning to anyone else. Nothing seemed to matter to him but pursuading Congress to buy and preserve his collection, for he continued to believe that this would help the Indians and the wilderness he loved. And for some reason taking the collection to England seemed to him to be the thing to do.

There were many problems for Catlin on the voyage, not least among them the grizzly bears. They were big and fierce. No sooner had they been placed aboard the ship than a sailor teased them by boxing with them through the iron bars of their cage. One of the bears promptly pulled the sailor's nose off with its sharp claws. Fortunately, the ship's surgeon was able to repair the sailor's nose to some extent, but the incident was a warning to Catlin of what traveling with two grizzly bears could mean. Afterward storms came up at sea, and the frightened growls of the grizzlies could be heard over the wild wind and waves. Catlin himself was exhausted and seasick before the end of the voyage, but at last the ship reached port in Liverpool, bears, paintings, tepees, peacepipes, and all, intact.

Catlin put on his exhibit in Manchester, Liverpool and London, but the crowds were not so large as he had hoped; worse, the offer from the British government to purchase the collection, that he had hoped for, did not come. His wife, his little girl, and a new baby daughter joined him, and Clara implored him to go home. He was just about to do that when a visitor changed his mind.

Catlin, although he had not accomplished any of his goals, had demonstrated an excellent sense of showmanship. The American exhibits had indicated to others that people would pay to see shows about Indians. Promoters had reasoned that if people were eager to see pictures of Indians, they might be even more eager to see real, live Indians. Out of this idea came "The Wild West Show," a unique, American variety of circus. The visitor who called on Catlin in London was a carnival showman. He had hoped to become rich by bringing a group of nine Ojibway Indians to England where they were to put on dances in English music halls. The Indians had proved to be less popular than the showman had anticipated and more expensive to feed and house than he had planned. So he had nine Indians he no longer wanted. He thought Catlin might want to put the Ojibways in his exhibition.

Catlin felt sorry for the Indians, and took them into his apartment at the hotel, to the alarm and excitement of the hotel keepers. He also put them in the exhibition. Among the nine were some women and children, and the group did add a great deal of interest to the display. Many more people flocked to see it, once it became known that the Indians were there.

Queen Victoria herself came, and her consort, Prince Albert. The Ojibways did a dance in Vauxhall Gardens, to the delight of the Queen and Prince; and the Ojibways, in return, enjoyed meeting the Queen. She was very polite to them and was especially interested in comparing ways of bringing up children with the squaws.

Because of the increased popularity of the exhibit, the Catlins spent three years in England. Everyone saw it and commented. Charles Dickens, for example, did not care for the Ojibways, and put his thoughts down in writing. He admitted, however, that Catlin was a pleasant enough fellow, in spite of his peculiar liking for Indians.

During the stay in England, two more children were born to the Catlin family, another little girl, and then a boy. Immediately after his son, also called George, was born, Catlin began making plans for a journey to France. The French that he had learned from Baptiste and Bogarde would come in handy there, for he planned to lecture to the crowds, just as he had in England and America. As the time for the journey came near, he often stayed up all night writing letters to Paris, arranging for exhibition and living space, advertising, and transportation. He seemed to have completely forgotten that he was an artist; he painted and drew nothing, and sometimes he even seemed to forget his original motive in coming abroad.

The truth was, he was desperate for money. Successful as the English exhibits had been, Catlin had spent far more for advertising and for space than he had taken in, and he did not have enough money for the return trip to New York. He hoped to manage his costs somewhat better in Paris, and make enough money to get home. The English exhibits had failed completely to make Congress act, and there seemed to be no point in staying abroad any longer.

Just as he was about to leave for Paris, when all arrangements had been made, the Ojibways left the show. They went back to America with the man who had brought them abroad originally. Apparently Catlin's use of the Indians had indicated that they were a successful entertainment group after all, and could be profitable. Even though Catlin was losing what had become an important part of his exhibition, he was relieved to see the Indians go, for food and lodging for them had been very expensive.

Then, to his surprise, and his wife's dismay, he acquired some more Indians. This time it was fourteen Ioways. They had been brought to London by a wealthy American gentleman who had decided to civilize them by showing them the great sights of Europe. Seeing a great many palaces and cathedrals, he was convinced, would make them cultured and refined. He considered his to be a great humanitarian mission. But it had been an utter failure; the Ioways missed their tepees and tall grass and saw nothing to admire in palaces and cathedrals, or in great cities where black smoke belched into the sky and turned it dark. When their sponsor saw that his students were doomed to remain raw, uncultured savages, he sighed, and regretfully admitted that those who said Indians were an inferior race were right. He set sail for home and left the Ioways behind, with no shelter but the cold, foggy, soot-filled streets of the London slums. They were worth no more to him than the many poor, ragged, abandoned children who filled the city's streets.

Their chief had met Catlin many years before. Somehow he discovered that Catlin was in London and came asking for help. He had no idea of how he and his people would live. Catlin took them in, explaining to Clara that perhaps they would bring financial success to the exhibit. Clara doubted this. She begged her husband to cancel his plans to go to Paris; she wanted to go home, even if it meant leaving the whole Indian exhibit in London.

But Catlin would not, or could not, go home. He took the exhibit, the Ioways, and his family to Paris. The king of France, Louis Philippe, welcomed the whole thing warmly. He was an eccentric man. He had fought in the French Revolution on the side of the common people. But then he had made enemies in the new republic and had spent several years in exile in the Lousiana Territory when it still belonged to France. Now, although he was known as "the Citizen King", he pleased neither those who were for royalty, nor those who were against it. Actually, he disliked being king. In exile in Lousiana he had gone down the Mississippi River on a raft, hearing the screeches of strange water birds, seeing trees hung with ghostly Spanish moss, and dreaming the days away in the humid, shimmering world of the great river. He would like to have spent his whole life being an explorer of the new world. He loved to read of the French explorers of America: Fathers Marquette and Joliet, and Robert La Salle. The Indians he had met on his Mississippi River journey had fascinated him. It was not surprising then that he was impressed with George Catlin, for Catlin had led exactly the life the King preferred.

Louis Philippe allowed Catlin to use the grand Egyptian wing of the Palace of the Louvre for the exhibit. Among the mummies and sphinxes of ancient Egypt, Catlin arranged his peacepipes and paintings and other treasures. The Ioways danced far into the night for the King of France and his guests in the formal gardens of the Tuileries. Windows in Paris flew open at the spine-chilling war whoops of the Ioways, while Louis Philippe begged the Indians to teach him some of their songs and steps. He talked enthusiastically with Catlin of purchasing the exhibt for the Louvre as a source of education for the French people. Catlin was tempted, but he refused because he still hoped and believed that his own country would buy the collection. He was corresponding with influential congressmen regularly. The King did not believe that this would happen and continued to talk about keeping the exhibit in France.

Winter was cold and damp that year in Paris. Three of the Ioway Indians and Clara Catlin all caught bad colds. Pneumonia rapidly developed, and within days all four were dead.

Catlin was devastated. He used up nearly all the

money he had left to send the remaining Ioways, and his wife's body, back to America. Left alone with his four little children, he canceled all of the exhibits he still had scheduled in France and waited each day for the mails to tell him that Congress had at last authorized the purchase of the collection.

Meanwhile, Louis Philippe commissioned Catlin to paint a series of pictures telling the story of Robert La Salle, the French explorer. Catlin, although he had little interest in this project, needed the money the king promised to pay. In fact, had the King again offered to buy the collection of Indain paintings and artifacts, Catlin might have been ready to sell. But now there was no definite offer, so the La Salle pictures were Catlin's only way of getting himself, his children, and his exhibit home.

Working on the pictures was not easy for Catlin. He had not painted much in a long time. And, furthermore, he had to be cook, nursemaid, and father to his children. It was all he could do to keep his little son from covering the La Salle painting with baby scrawls. But Catlin finally discovered he could keep the little boy enthralled for hours by telling him exciting tales of his adventures among the Indians. Catlin drew funny pictures of himself, Baptiste, and Bogarde as they traveled down the long Missouri River, the tame war eagle leading the way. Catlin even promised the boy that he would take him on such an adventure, just the two of them, some day. The king gave the little boy a beautiful drum, just like the ones the king's own drummer boys used. And when Catlin grew tired

*Little
Blackfoot
boy*

of telling stories, he had the little boy march, beating his drum, through the Paris apartment. As for the girls, he made a game of teaching them to wash his paintbrushes. For he himself had no time to stop painting.

Then suddenly, the little drummer boy caught a cold. Within a few days, he, like his mother and the three Ioways, was dead of pneumonia. And whatever the infection was that had spread through the Catlin household, taking five lives, it affected Catlin, too. He had a severe and persistent ear infection that kept him constantly dizzy and feverish, and he realized that it was destroying his hearing.

It seemed then as if nothing worse could happen. But more was in store. One night, what had begun as a street demonstration demanding various election reforms, broke out into violence. Catlin's friend, King Louis Philippe, was immediately smuggled out of France before the mob could get to him and take him to the guillotine to be beheaded. With that, of course, Catlin knew he would never be paid for the La Salle paintings, which, by that time, were nearly finished. Furthermore, his own life and the lives of his daughters were in danger because of his friendship with the King.

Somehow, he and the children, and what was left of his exhibit, escaped to London. The studio in Paris was broken into after he had fled, and the paintings he had left behind were destroyed.

Then, in England, he heard good news. At last Congress was ready to puchase his collection. Catlin, overjoyed and confident, borrowed money to live on and waited to hear more. But still it was not to be. Fighting broke out between the United States and Mexico, and the bill to purchase Catlin's material was put aside. The government needed the money to buy guns and pay soldiers. For Catlin and his children, that was a disaster. He had no money at all; his debts were overwhelming; he hardly dared open his door, for the only people who ever called were creditors coming to collect the money he owed them.

When help came, it was not entirely what Catlin would have wished. His brother-in-law, who had often warned him that his ambitions were hopeless, arrived in England and took the little girls home with him. They were, after all, his own sister's children. He intended, he said, to rear the girls as if they were his own. Catlin was to have as little to do with them as possible, so that they would not grow up to be as irresponsible as he was. Catlin could not blame his brother-in-law. He blamed only himself for all the terrible things that happened to his family.

Soon after the children were gone, a wealthy American named Joseph Harrison paid Catlin's debts. In return, he took the Indian collection home to America with him. He had seen it years before and found it very interesting; once it was his, he stored it in a boiler factory he owned in Philadelphia.

*Uraguay medicine man*

# chapter eight

There was nothing left of Catlin's life's work, of his family, or even of his hearing. And it seemed to him that there was nothing left for him in the United States either. So he returned to Paris, where he lived under a different name. He was deeply ashamed of all that had happened. And no one who had known him would have recognized the tattered, silent man who prowled the Paris Streets selling an occasional water-color to tourists and Parisians, as the handsome and charming George Catlin, who had thrilled the world with his exhibits.

Catlin had become so deaf that conversation was difficult for him. His only pleasure was reading. In the Bibliotheque National he read strange and wonder-filled descriptions of the Indians of South America, as the early Spanish explorers had seen them. Soon thoughts of the tribes living in South America came to haunt George Catlin, as his dream of seeing the Plains Indians in their natural state had once held him. There was no reason not to go, so he became determined to see South America and paint the Indians there. With this new reason for living, and still under an alias, he sailed for South America. Perhaps in South America he could even find a clue to solve the questions that had tormented and puzzled him. Who were these people? Where had they come from?

In Venezuela he met a man willing to travel with him. Few people would have been foolish enough to go on one of George Catlin's wild journeys into the wilderness, but this man had, like Catlin, nothing left to lose. He was a tall, strong, young black man, a runaway slave from Cuba. His name was Cesar; and together, Cesar and Catlin set off into the unknown lands of South America.

Years passed, and no one heard of George Catlin. People still remembered him, and there were rumors that he was in South America. The United States government finally sent a small expedition to look for him. But the expedition did not find him. So he was assumed to be dead, and he was soon forgotten by the public. Meanwhile his paintings and war bonnets and peacepipes and tall tepees gathered dust in Harrison's boiler works in Philadelphia.

But he was not dead. He and Cesar were wandering through the high Andes Mountains of Peru, and among the primitive tribesmen of Patagonia, among the great jungles of the Amazon River. He was hearing more legends of a great flood and seeing ruins of ancient and extensive civilizations—Inca, Maya, and Aztec—now vanished forever. He was comparing the Mandan flood myths with others he was hearing, and wondering still where the Indians had come from. He had begun to think that there might have been a vast Indian civilization, perhaps the oldest in the world, that had been destroyed by flood and was hidden somewhere beneath the sea. He looked at rocks for clues and wandered on and drew and painted.

For five years he and Cesar wandered from North to South, even returning through Mexico to the United States, where Catlin painted some of the Indians of the Southwest. He and Cesar hunted pink flamingos along the Amazon, listening to the screeches of parrots and monkeys, and narrowly escaped a hungry jaguar's claws. At last the two of them made their way onto a ship that was sailing the Pacific Ocean from Lima, Peru, to Vancouver Island, Canada. Catlin wanted to see the Indians of the Northwest Coast and the Eskimos. And he remembered that his old friend, General William Clark, had reached the Pacific Ocean on foot and returned. It seemed to Catlin that he could make his way back across the great bluffs and prairies of the West into what remained of the lands of the Sioux, Crows, Blackfeet, Assiniboins, and the place where the Mandans would never sunbathe again.

In Vancouver he and Cesar visited the great log lodges of the Kwakiutls and watched them carve totem poles and war canoes, and cut up giant fresh-killed whales. Because Catlin had long since lost his easel somewhere in the jungles of the Amazon, he simply leaned his canvases and wooden boards against Cesar's straight back as he painted, while Cesar watched the sights that his strange companion led him to.

Then one day, Cesar left. He had decided that five years of travel were enough. There was a girl in Venezuela who loved him, and he had decided to marry her. Both men cried when they parted, for they had seen and done and shared many things together, and now they would never see each other again.

Then, somehow, George Catlin found his way across the mountains and plains of the West. But he did not stay in the eastern United States. Instead he sailed for Paris, and eventually moved on to Brussels, where he led a strange and secretive life. He was a man of great mystery to his neighbors. He told them nothing of himself, and refused to speak when people asked him about his family. He described himself only as "the friend of the Indians."

Catlin had not gone empty-handed to his new home in Brussels. Besides painting South American Indians, he had done a great deal of writing in his five years in South America. Now he published a book for boys about his adventures, which he illustrated with pictures he had made. Some of the stories were the ones that had amused his little son that cold winter in Paris. Now they brought enjoyment to older boys as well. The book was praised and admired by everyone who read it; many liked it even better than *Robinson Crusoe* and other well-loved adventure tales. It sold well and the royalties were substantial. For the first time in many years Catlin earned some money, more than the small amounts he had subsisted on by selling pictures to whoever would buy.

The first book was followed by a second, a strange little volume he had written in South America. It was filled with peculiar little pen and ink drawings, and it was hand-lettered in a most unusual way. Among other things it told of the healthy ways that Indians breathed, and it told of the terrible things that could happen to people who didn't breathe properly. One man who diligently followed its good advice and tried his best to breathe properly, was a mathematics professor at Oxford University. Whether he learned much from the book isn't certain; but it is thought that when this man himself wrote a book, the comical little drawings in George Catlin's book may have influenced him; for he drew funny pictures very like Catlin's and lettered his book in much the same style. That book was *Alice in Wonderland.*

In 1870 George Catlin went back to New York. He was, for the first time in many years, successful, and he wanted to see his daughters. They were grown by then, and he was old. Perhaps because of his success as an author, he felt he could face them without shame.

While he was in New York the thing that he had wanted for years and years happened. The Smithsonian Institution in Washington indicated that it would like to exhibit his pictures, perhaps permanently, and show some of his collection.

The paintings were hung, but the Indian artifacts had been too long in the boiler factory. Mice and moths had nibbled away at the fur robes and the war

83

bonnets. A fire, and the smoke and water that went with it, had damaged other things, including many of the paintings. The Indian treasures that Catlin had carried across the world were filled with dust and smoke and mildew, and nothing remained of their former beauty.

It was too late in other ways, too. All the things Catlin had feared would happen had come to pass. The Sioux had grown to hate and mistrust all white men. The hatred of the Arikaras was mild compared with the bitter feelings and ferocity that existed between white man and Sioux. Fighting between Indians and white settlers went on constantly, and yet the settlers went west in ever greater numbers. In battles with the Indians, the settlers were usually the losers. But the United States Army was more successful. The tribes were forced to move onto reservations. The buffalo began decreasing rapidly, because their grazing lands were so diminished, and because the white men were shooting too many. In fact, a general bounty was placed on buffalo by the government in order to hasten their disappearance. For in this way the Indians could perhaps be done away with. This reasoning seemed correct. The Indians saw the creatures they depended upon for food, sport, joy, and everything that was important in their lives, disappear, and they themselves began to vanish. Catlin's paintings told of happier times on the great plains, times that seemed far back in the past. Perhaps it was for this reason that the Smithsonian felt it needed them. They recorded an America that would not be seen again.

George Catlin died in December of 1872. He died still uncertain of what would become of his paintings, but he need not have worried. The heirs of Joseph Harrison gave the paintings to the Smithsonian, where they are today among the greatest treasures of that museum. In fact, some of them, some of the finest, returned recently to Paris, to decorate the ambassador's residence there, for Catlin, the artist, has always been admired in France, as one of the finest American painters.

Catlin's daughters gave his drawings, which they inherited, to the American Museum of Natural History and to the New York Historical Society. For the American Museum of Natural History they are valued documents in the anthropology collections, for they give information that was never recorded elsewhere about the life and customs of the Plains Indians.

After Catlin's death serious fighting broke out between the Sioux, who had as yet not been forced onto a reservation, and white gold miners who forced their way into the Sioux-held Black Hills of South Dakota; many miners and Sioux alike were killed. So the army decided all Sioux should be forced onto a reservation. Two important chiefs, Sitting Bull and Crazy Horse, refused to lead their people to the reservation. In 1876 General George Armstrong Custer led an attack against Crazy Horse and his warriors. Custer and all his men were killed, but nevertheless, the Sioux were doomed. They were rounded up by the army and put on a reservation. The last of the great hunters and warriors of the plains had been subdued, and where the buffalo had wandered, cattle, and wheat and corn could grow. Catlin's dream of a hunting ground for the Indians was forever lost.

Today, for people who want to know about the vanished Indians of the plains, Catlin's paintings tell a great deal. But they are something more. Catlin learned to paint with great speed; he felt a deep love for his subject, and his paintings capture with color and spontaneity the essence of a world that was as fresh and beautiful and bright, as sun and wind on the prairie.